THIS IS NOT HEAVEN

Making Sense of the Pleasure and Pain of Life

– and Thriving

By Jill Bowman

Jill Bowman

This Is Not Heaven

Dedication

To my parents and my parents-in-law
who pointed me toward a good path.
To my husband, my fellow truth-seeker,
who has made me more brave.
To the many, many people who have
publicly and courageously shared their
wild stories in a way that would reach me.

Jill Bowman

Contents

When you look at the house on the cover of this book, what do you see? Do you see a life of unimaginable luxury? Prestige and respect? Financial security? Many would. But not all. Some would see a vast, lonely space. Unending square footage to maintain. A financial burden.

Everyone has their own perspective on life - what's yours? Does it give you hope? Joy? Or fear? Anger? Anxiety?

What if I told you that hope and joy can be your default perspective of life here on earth, no matter what your circumstances?

I know, that's a bold claim, but hear me out. All it takes is time...do you want to take the time to discover and really take hold of a life of hope, and joy? If you do, friend, then I have a gift for you, and I am so happy you want to receive it!

You see, life holds before us the promise of being like heaven. Oh, there is beauty. Majesty, even. Towering mountains, rushing rivers, trees waving in the wind, hawks gliding across the sky. Crashing ocean waves, sun-baked sand. Playful puppies, cooing babies, your best friend's smile. That great neighbor who helps you out when you need it. Your wife's eyes, your child's giggle. A rewarding career. A comfortable home. A beautiful car. Fantastic vacations.

But there is darkness, too. Earthquakes, famines, floods, tsunamis. A spectrum of diseases. Scarcity. Thirst for power, war. Fear, anger, the need to control. Hatred. Violence.

So many people come to the conclusion that there could not be a loving Creator, because he would not make a world like this, with so much injustice, where children are abused, where evil prospers.

An easy conclusion to jump to – but dead wrong. This is not heaven. There is more at work here than most people realize. And the more time you spend discovering our Creator's perspective, the more the pleasure and pain of this world will make sense.

Friend, I care about you. You are a work of art, a masterpiece. You have potential to achieve, and when you achieve it, it will be the most amazing and satisfying experience, more than you could have ever dreamed.

But the road is narrow, and few find it.

Do you have that sinking feeling that there is more to life? More to life on earth?

Follow that.

Follow me on that line of thinking.

I have found treasure, a treasure that is hidden in plain sight. A treasure that has made me rich beyond what I could imagine. This treasure is available to you as well – you only need to take the time to unwrap it. This book is a 'quick start' guide to help you do just that.

So Much Suffering

"I have told you these things so that in me you will have peace. In this world you will have trouble, but take heart! I have overcome the world." (John 16:33)

Did you know Jesus said this? It's not one of those things that pop into our minds when tragedy strikes. Sometimes we are just overwhelmed with pain in that moment. We want a powerful protector to bring safety and make all the pain go away.

But when tragedy strikes, this is what we should remember: this is not heaven. God is not surprised. This place is full of people with the freedom to choose their own path. Light or darkness. Love or hate. Generosity or selfishness. Courage or fear. Building up or tearing down. Honor or shame.

But not all choose to take up the position that is offered to them, as beloved son or daughter in the kingdom of God, doing the good works that he has planned for them to do (Ephesians 2:10), and trusting him to provide their needs as he promised (Matthew 6). On earth, we are tempted to build our own kingdoms, take what we can get, drink and be merry for tomorrow, we die. That temptation is embraced by many, and it leads to sin, degradation, and death, for ourselves, and for those around us.

But we have a rescuer! Jesus came here willingly to die, to pay the debt that was owed for all our crimes, so that we could legally walk out of the jail that we deserve to be in, and into the freedom to reach the full potential God has for our lives.

When we decide to find out what it means to live as a beloved son or daughter of God here on earth, we will still have to deal with dysfunctional people (ourselves included!), but he teaches us compassion for ourselves and others, gives us patience with each other when we need it, and shows us the way to make a world that's more like heaven, if we would all encourage one another to make it that way!

Did you know that Jesus said some pretty radical things? "Love your enemies." Who can do that? "If your hand causes you to sin, cut it off." Wow, that's serious! "No one who loves their family more than Me is worthy of Me." What? Isn't love the highest goal? How could loving someone be wrong?

This is why in the introduction I asked you to take time to understand God's ways, the ways of Hope and Joy. His ways are higher than our ways. Love is not a knee jerk reaction, it's deliberate action in the best interest of the object of your love. To love someone is not to possess them, it is to lay down your life for them.

So why does God give people the freedom to choose to hurt one another? He created us to be able to choose to love, or not, because only willing love is real love. And in giving us real freedom to choose, some will choose not to love...and all the people around that person have to deal with their choice not to love, not to trust, not to have faith, not to honor their Heavenly Father who wants nothing more than to love them, provide for them, accomplish something together on earth, and welcome them into their place he has prepared for them in heaven.

So what do we do with the pain that we experience here on earth? We bring it to the foot of the cross. We kneel at Jesus' feet, we cry, we scream, even. He knows. He puts his arms around us. He has felt the pain of loss, betrayal, violence. He longs for the day ahead, when "He will wipe away every tear from their eyes, and death shall be no more, neither shall there be mourning, nor crying, nor pain anymore, for the former things have passed away." (Revelation 21:4)

The Power of Generosity

The point is this: whoever sows sparingly will also reap sparingly, and whoever sows bountifully will also reap bountifully. Each one must give as he has decided in his heart, not reluctantly or under compulsion, for God loves a cheerful giver. (2 Corinthians 9: 6-7)

"I the Lord do not change. So you, the descendants of Jacob, are not destroyed. Ever since the time of your ancestors you have turned away from my decrees and have not kept them. Return to me, and I will return to you," says the Lord Almighty.

"But you ask, 'How are we to return?'

"Will a mere mortal rob God? Yet you rob me.'

"But you ask, 'How are we robbing you?'

"In tithes and offerings. You are under a curse—your whole nation—because you are robbing me. Bring the whole tithe into the storehouse, that there may be food in my house. Test me in this," says the Lord Almighty, "and see if I will not throw open the floodgates of heaven and pour out so much blessing that there will not be room enough to store it. I will prevent pests from devouring your crops, and the vines in your fields will not drop their fruit before it is ripe," says the Lord Almighty. "Then all the nations will call you blessed, for yours will be a delightful land," says the Lord Almighty. (Malachi 3:6-12)

God created everything from nothing. With him there is no scarcity, nothing is in short supply. With us, not so much. Few of us have had more than enough of the resources we need in our lives.

He wants us to step out of our scarcity and into his abundance. He wants to provide for us. It is part of being his child!

So why does he want us to give to him, if he has everything? Because IT CHANGES US, AND IT CHANGES THE WORLD. It helps us become people who reflect his generous and brave and trusting heart. It wins people over who are stuck in a mindset that they have to steal what they need. We become the wonderful community he has intended us to be!

How do I start? Give 10% of your income to your church that is teaching the truth of God's word and providing for the needs of its members and reaching out to the local community to help. If you don't attend a church, find one. If you can't find one locally, but you find yourself being fed spiritually with solid teaching from a church that is online, give to that church, and try to find ways to be a part of life with that church (maybe inviting friends to watch with you in your home, etc.) Give where you feel led to help, where God's name is glorified and people are helping others to thrive. There are multitudes of choices: prison ministries, homeless shelters, domestic abuse shelters, and more. Not sure if you can trust them? Look for the ECFA seal, which will tell you that they are audited by the Evangelical Council on Financial Accountability, who reviews their handling of finances and compares that to their mission statement that they put forward to donors.

Does 10% seem like a lot? Start with a smaller percentage, and ask God to help you work up to 10%. God honors baby steps in the right direction!

"Don't store up treasures here on earth, where moths eat them and rust destroys them, and where thieves break in and steal. Store your treasures in heaven, where moths and rust cannot destroy, and thieves do not break in and steal. Wherever your treasure is, there the desires of your heart will also be.

Your eye is like a lamp that provides light for your body. When your eye is healthy, your whole body is filled with light. But when your eye is unhealthy, your whole body is filled with darkness. And if the light you think you have is actually darkness, how deep that darkness is!

No one can serve two masters. For you will hate one and love the other; you will be devoted to one and despise the other. You cannot serve God and be enslaved to money.

That is why I tell you not to worry about everyday life—whether you have enough food and drink, or enough clothes to wear. Isn't life more than food, and your body more than clothing? Look at the birds. They don't plant or harvest or store food in barns, for your heavenly Father feeds them. And aren't you far more valuable to him than they are? Can all your worries add a single moment to your life?

And why worry about your clothing? Look at the lilies of the field and how they grow. They don't work or make their clothing, yet Solomon in all his glory was not dressed as beautifully as they are. And if God cares so wonderfully for wildflowers that are here today and thrown into the fire tomorrow, he will certainly care for you. Why do you have so little faith?

So don't worry about these things, saying, 'What will we eat? What will we drink? What will we wear?' These things dominate the thoughts of unbelievers, but your heavenly Father already knows all your needs. Seek the Kingdom of God above all else, and live righteously, and he will give you everything you need. (Words of Jesus, Matthew 6:19-33)

What is Faith?

To some, faith is knowledge. A belief system. But faith in the God of the Bible is a relationship. And relationships take time! What are we to do when time is in short supply? And how do we build a relationship with God, who is unseen?

For many of us, it seems like there are not enough hours in the day, or days in the week. We are needed by those around us. Others can't do what we do. Life is moving faster every day, expectations increasing. More than ever, we need the strength that is available to us through a relationship with God. But how can we access that?

The rest of this book is a practical guide to help you break through the barrier of having little time to connect with God, and help you to hear his heart for you and those you love. Learn how to find joy even in the struggles of life. Learn how to find the way to the satisfying and fulfilling life that God wants to give you.

Taking a Moment

Imagine God as your new boss. He is unlike any boss you have ever had. He cares about you. He wants you to be successful, and is able and willing to provide what you need in order to reach your full potential. Not only that, he sees potential in you that you have not yet discovered for yourself, and he knows how to develop that potential. He guarantees that his employees will be supplied with the food and clothing they need, as long as they are committed to following his leadership.

Will you take some moments in your day to turn your attention toward God, like you would a valued mentor? Here are some ways you can connect with God in the moment:

❖ Explore your favorite music app, looking for Christian artists – there are some artists in your favorite genre! Favorite the songs that remind you of God's faithfulness and give wisdom, and go back to them often.

❖ Have a scripture calendar on your desk, or in your car, or somewhere you spend time every day. Read the verse daily.

❖ Sign up for daily devotional emails or "verses of the day" text messages or notifications. They are available from many websites and apps: BibleGateway.com, YouVersion Bible app, InTouch Ministries, Ransomed Heart, Faith Radio, the list is endless!

- ❖ Tune in to Christian radio and television programs or podcasts. Find one you like and tune in regularly.
- ❖ Carry this guide with you. Read when you are pumping gas, waiting in line, eating lunch, whenever you have a moment!
- ❖ Be alert for moments that your attention is not required by life's responsibilities. Take a breath. Take that moment to appreciate something good that God has done—the sunshine, the rain, your health, your family, the comfortable chair you are sitting in—and thank God for it!

Taking an Hour

Relationships tend to remain surface level if they are only given moments at a time. Sometimes we need to devote some time to really hear each other, really connect. Many people spend the first hour or so of the day with God, their Bible, their journal, and a cup of coffee. Don't feel guilty if that sounds like an impossible task, just do what you can do. Start with once!

There is much to discover about God's personality by reading the Bible. The first five books are the same books that people of Jewish faith call the Torah. Genesis is the first book, and it contains the stories of Adam and Eve, Cain and Abel (their sons), the Tower of Babel, Noah and the Great Flood, Abraham, Isaac, Jacob, and Joseph of "Technicolor Dreamcoat" fame. Through these stories you can learn how God wants to have relationship with his people. Exodus contains the story of Moses, and the Israelites leaving captivity in Egypt, crossing the Red Sea which was miraculously split for them to cross. Psalms, near the middle of the Bible, is the book of songs written by King David, who was called a man after God's heart. He wrote songs of praise for God's provision and protection, in which many people find hope and encouragement. Next, Proverbs is a book written by King Solomon, David's son, who was known for his wisdom. Those are all books of the Old Testament.

The New Testament begins with the four gospels, Matthew, Mark, Luke, and John. These four books are written by disciples and close followers of Jesus, and give the account of Jesus' life from their perspectives. Acts tells about how the church grew after Jesus' resurrection and ascension to heaven. Many of the remaining books are letters written by Paul to various churches. Often he wrote them from prison, and yet he encouraged people in their faith and gave guidance on how God wants us to live, and to treat each other.

Start with a book that sounds interesting, and read it slowly enough to let it sink in. Enjoy your time with God. Get to know him. He does amazing things!

The remainder of this book is designed to give you a glimpse into God's heart for you, his purposes for life, and his plans for your future. There are questions at the end of each chapter to help you apply the verses to your life. I hope that you are strengthened and energized for life by these verses as I am! Enjoy!

The World According to God

God made this world. He could have made it any way he wanted to. Sure, at first glance, there are a lot of things wrong with it. You might think he, being perfect, could have done a lot better.

But don't take one look at the world and decide he's not loving, or powerful enough, to trust with your life. Don't dwell on the pain you've suffered at the hands of others and hold it between you and God, as a wall.

Reach out to him. Read his Word, his history of love for you. Get to know him by reading the stories of Moses, of Joseph, of David. He knows your heart, what will satisfy you in this life. Seek him, and that is what you will find.

"For I know the plans I have for you," declares the Lord, "plans to prosper you and not to harm you, plans to give you a hope and a future. Then you will call on me and pray to me, and I will listen to you. You will seek me and find me when you seek me with all your heart." (Jeremiah 29:11-13)

One thing God has spoken,
    two things I have heard:"
Power belongs to you, God,
    and with you, Lord, is unfailing love";
and, "You reward everyone
    according to what they have done." (Psalm 62:11-12)

Joseph, had this to say to his brothers, who had sold him into slavery years earlier: "Don't be afraid. Am I in the place of God? You intended to harm me, but God intended it for good to accomplish what is now being done, the saving of many lives." (Genesis 50:19-20)

And we know that in all things God works for the good of those who love Him, who have been called according to His purpose. (Romans 8:28)

The Parable of the Weeds
Jesus told them another parable: "The kingdom of heaven is like a man who sowed good seed in his field. But while everyone was sleeping, his enemy came and sowed weeds among the wheat, and went away. When the wheat sprouted and formed heads, then the weeds also appeared.
    The owner's servants came to him and said, "Sir, didn't you sow good seed in your field? Where then did the weeds come from?"
    "An enemy did this," he replied.
    The servants asked him, "Do you want us to go and pull them up?"
    "No," he answered, "because while you are pulling the weeds, you may root up the wheat with them. Let both grow together until the harvest. At that time I will tell the harvesters: First collect the weeds and tie them in bundles to be burned; then gather the wheat and bring it into my barn." (Matthew 13:24-30)

Food For Thought: *Do you blame God for some bad thing in your life or in the life of someone you care about? Tell God about your pain. Ask for His help to cope and to heal. If you feel led, pray that He would give you some understanding regarding the situation, or perhaps help you to see how some good might have come out of the situation.*

You Are Valuable

You are not valuable because you are attractive, smart, strong, talented, rich, funny, athletic, or friendly. You are valuable because you are God's creation.

He put you together himself, purposefully giving you strengths so that you could help others, and weaknesses so that others can help you and be of value to you. He did not create people to be independent, but to be interdependent.

If you ever feel less valuable than another person, banish that thought, because it is not from God.

Seek his kingdom and discover his purpose for giving you the abilities you possess. Accept your weaknesses as gifts from him, and allow them to teach you many things.

For you created my inmost being; you knit me together in my mother's womb. I praise you because I am fearfully and wonderfully made. (Psalm 139:13-14a)

Your kingdom is an everlasting kingdom,
 and your dominion endures through all generations.
The LORD is trustworthy in all he promises
 and faithful in all he does.
The LORD upholds all who fall
 and lifts up all who are bowed down. (Psalm 145:13-14)

The Lord delights in those who fear Him, who put their hope in His unfailing love. (Psalm 147:11)

The Parable of the Lost Sheep
"What do you think? If a man owns a hundred sheep, and one of them wanders away, will he not leave the ninety-nine on the hills and go to look for the one that wandered off? And if he finds it, I tell you the truth, he is happier about that one sheep than about the ninety-nine that did not wander off. In the same way your Father in heaven is not willing that any of these little ones should be lost." (Matthew 18:12-14)

Food For Thought: *What strengths and abilities do you have? What weaknesses? Honestly look at yourself. Ask God to help you to know and accept yourself as He made you.*

Come As You Are, Then Grow in Grace

You do not have to get your act together before approaching God's throne. There is nothing in your life that you have to fix, no desire or temptation you have to rid yourself of, so that you will make yourself acceptable to him.

Do not pridefully think that you could make yourself holy and pure—that is his job. Not even Mother Teresa could earn her way into his kingdom, because she, like all people, was born with a sinful heart, without the spiritual life of Christ.

All you need to do is to believe that God sent his Son, Jesus, born of a virgin, holy and sinless, the only Man born spiritually alive. Believe that He made the way for you where you were not able.

Let go of trying to be good enough, and accept His gift of His perfect righteousness. Put it on like clothing, covering your sin, and you will be acceptable to God.

Do good deeds as an expression of love for God, not motivated by a desire to earn his favor, but because you are inspired by who he is, and because you are grateful for the love and care you have received from him. He will embrace you as his child, and he will be your faithful and dependable Father.

For God so loved the world that He gave His one and only Son, that whoever believes in Him shall not perish but have everlasting life. (John 3:16)

Therefore no one will be declared righteous in God's sight by the works of the law; rather, through the law we become conscious of our sin. (Romans 3:20)

This righteousness from God comes through faith in Jesus Christ to all who believe. There is no difference, for all have sinned and fall short of the glory of God, and are justified freely by his grace through the redemption that came by Christ Jesus. (Romans 3:22-24)

At that time the disciples came to Jesus and asked, "Who is the greatest in the kingdom of heaven?" He called a little child and had him stand among them. And he said: "I tell you the truth, unless you change and become like little children, you will never enter the kingdom of heaven. Therefore, whoever humbles himself like this child is the greatest in the kingdom of heaven. And whoever welcomes a little child like this in my name welcomes me." (Matthew 18:1-5)

Do not merely listen to the word, and so deceive yourselves. Do what it says. Anyone who listens to the word but does not do what it says is like someone who looks at his face in a mirror and, after looking at himself, goes away and immediately forgets what he looks like. But whoever looks intently into the perfect law that gives freedom, and continues in it—not forgetting what they have heard, but doing it—they will be blessed in what they do. (James 1:22-25)

Food For Thought: *Have you been holding back your life and heart from God until __________ (you fill in the blank)? Ask God to help you to understand what's holding you back, and how he really views that situation.*

Plans, Goals & Dreams

God created you with many talents and abilities. You may have goals and dreams for your future based on your plans to use those talents and abilities for earthly success.

But will you take a moment to try to see your life from God's perspective? Will you reflect on the talents and abilities he has given you, and imagine the wonderful possibilities for your life that he may have planned?

If you would join him, if you would honor him by giving these abilities to him and asking him to lead you in your use of them, you will be taking the first step in a wonderful journey.

On this journey you will learn to follow him, and you will enable him to lead you into opportunities to use your abilities in a most fulfilling way, in ways you have not dreamed of.

But those who hope in the Lord will renew their strength. They will soar on wings like eagles; they will run and not grow weary, they will walk and not be faint. (Isaiah 40:31)

Since ancient times no one has heard,
    no ear has perceived,
no eye has seen any God besides you,
    who acts on behalf of those who wait for him.
(Isaiah 64:4)

Unless the Lord builds the house, its builders labor in vain.
(Psalm 127:1)

Therefore since Christ suffered in his body, arm yourselves also with the same attitude, because he who has suffered in his body is done with sin. As a result, he does not live the rest of his earthly life for evil human desires, but rather for the will of God. (1 Peter 4:1-2)

Then he said to them all: "If anyone would come after me, he must deny himself and take up his cross [the task that God has for you] daily and follow me. For whoever wants to save his life will lose it, but whoever loses his life for me will same it. What good is it for a man to gain the whole world, and yet lose or forfeit his very self?" (Luke 9:23-25)

Food For Thought: *What task might God have for you to complete? Consider your abilities, and prayerfully ask God to show you how you might join Him in His work. Don't think that your life has to change drastically overnight in order for God to be pleased with you. Think of yourself as a work in progress. The actions you take that are motivated by love for God and a desire to honor Him are actions that will bear fruit in your life. (John 15)*

#1 On Your To Do List

God made you for a reason. You are not a mistake or an accident. God made you deliberately. He loves you just as you are.

The thing he cares most about is his relationship with his people. It is his hope that you will love him, trust him, and depend on him.

How can I repay the Lord for all his goodness to me? I will lift up the cup of salvation and call on the name of the Lord. (Psalms 116:12-13)

Delight yourself in the Lord and He will give you the desires of your heart. (Psalm 37:4)

But God demonstrates his own love for us in this: While we were still sinners, Christ died for us. (Romans 5:8)

"Teacher, which is the greatest commandment in the Law?"

Jesus replied, "'Love the Lord your God with all your heart, and with all your soul, and with all your mind.' This is the first and greatest commandment." (Matthew 22:36-38)

Food For Thought: *What does this commandment mean to you? Is it strange to you that God would ask us to love him with our hearts, souls, and minds? Many people see God as a ruler or a judge, and find it strange that Almighty God would command love ahead of obedience. However, relationship with God is the reason we were created. Pray that God would help you to understand how precious you are to Him, and that He would help your love for Him grow.*

#2 On Your To Do List

For many reasons, God created people in such a way that they need each other. Seeing people living in harmony and caring for each other brings him great joy.

You will know him better when you love and care for those around you for his sake.

Therefore, as God's chosen people, holy and dearly loved, clothe yourselves with compassion, kindness, humility, gentleness and patience. Bear with each other and forgive whatever grievances you may have against one another. Forgive as the Lord forgave you. (Colossians 3:12-13)

And whatever you do, whether in word or deed, do it all in the name of the Lord Jesus, giving thanks to God the Father through him. Wives, submit yourselves to your husbands, for you have been created to be your husband's essential companion in life. Husbands, love your wives and do not be harsh with them. Children, obey your parents in everything, for this pleases the Lord. Fathers, do not embitter your children, or they will become discouraged. Slaves, obey your earthly masters in everything; and do it, not only when their eye is on you and to curry their favor, but with sincerity of heart and reverence for the Lord. Whatever you do, work at it with all your heart, as working for the Lord, not for human masters, since you know that you will receive an inheritance from the Lord as a reward. It is the Lord Christ you are serving. Anyone who does wrong will be repaid for their wrongs, and there is no favoritism. (Colossians 3:17-4:1)

Then Jesus came to them and said, "All authority in heaven and on earth has been given to me. Therefore, go and make disciples of all nations, baptizing them in the name of the Father and of the Son and of the Holy Spirit, and teaching them to obey everything I have commanded you. And surely I am with you always, to the very end of the age." (Matthew 28:18-20)

"And the second [greatest commandment] is like it; 'Love your neighbor as yourself.' All Law and the Prophets hang on these two commandments." (Matthew 22:39-40)

Food For Thought: *How do we love those around us? Often that love can be in ways we think of as small...donating some clothing to those in need, checking up on an elderly neighbor, helping out with the children's ministry at church, going with a group to sing carols at a hospital in December. Other times, the decisions we make in response to our own circumstances will give a testimony to those around us. Just by trusting in God's promises, and stepping out in faith that God will do what He says, lives of those around us can be changed. Not everyone is called to go far away lands to reach people for the gospel. Some of us are called to be store clerks, and office workers, managers, and public servants, quietly living out our faith, helping our neighbors, and loving our God. God can use anyone who is willing to allow His love to shine through them.*

Think Outside the Box

You have heard people say that God is everywhere. You may have read it in his word. But do you believe it? Do you believe when you're sitting at your desk at work that you can stop and talk to him, heart to heart, and he will hear you? That he will listen, and it will make a difference?

Can you imagine that he might be interested in what you can do together, you and God, in the part of his world you're in?

He created you, but he also gave you free will. Your heart is yours to give. Giving yourself to anyone or anything other than him may satisfy you temporarily, but will not truly fulfill your heart. I hope that you choose to invite him into your days, so that you can experience the depth of his love for you, and the wonder of life as he meant for it to be lived.

He is real. Believe it. Step out in faith. Let the fact that he is real change your response to the world around you.

Remain in Me and I will remain in you. No branch can bear fruit by itself; it must remain in the vine. Neither can you bear fruit unless you remain in Me. I am the vine; you are the branches. If a man remains in Me and I in him, he will bear much fruit. (John 15:4-5a)

Trust in the LORD with all your heart
    and lean not on your own understanding;
in all your ways submit to him,

and he will make your paths straight. (Proverbs 3:5-6)

For the message of the cross is foolishness to those who are perishing, but to us who are being saved it is the power of God. (1 Corinthians 1:18)

Do not conform any longer to the pattern of this world, but be transformed by the renewing of your mind. Then you will be able to test and approve what God's will is--his good, pleasing, and perfect will. (Romans 12:2)

We have not received the spirit of the world but the Spirit who is from God, that we may understand what God has freely given us. The man without the Spirit does not accept the things that come from the Spirit of God, for they are foolishness to him, and he cannot understand them, because they are spiritually discerned. (1 Corinthians 2:12 & 14).

Knowledge puffs up, but love builds up. (1 Corinthians 8:1)

Do not worry about your life, what you will eat or drink; or about your body, what you will wear. Is not life more important than food, and the body more important than clothes? Look at the birds of the air; they do not sow or reap or store away in barns, and yet their heavenly Father feeds them. Are you not much more valuable than they? Who of you by worrying can add a single hour to his life? (Matthew 6:25-27)

Food For Thought: *Try to see the world through God's eyes. Pray for God to help you to discern right from wrong, the beauty of holiness from the ugliness of sin, His ways from our ways. Ask Him to guard your mind from false ideas, show you the truth, and give you wisdom to make good decisions when those moments come.*

$$$

The earth is the Lord's and everything in it (Psalms 24:1). So why does he ask you to give when he could surely take care of the needs himself?

He asks you to give because it's good for you. You'll understand him better. You'll see your own faith in action.

Seek his leading as you decide how the resources within your control will be used. When you make a habit of considering his will for the resources under your control, he will be able to trust you with more, knowing you will make wise decisions and seek his guidance.

When you give for his sake, you will release his blessing on your life that he longs to give to you. You will gain a new perspective of your life, a new hope, a realization of his abundance, and strong faith in his promise to provide for your needs.

How can you experience his power in your life if you always refuse to depend on him to provide? Step out in faith and spend your money the way you know he wants you to!

Honor the Lord with your wealth, with the first fruits of all your crops; then your barns will be filled to overflowing, and your vats will brim over with new wine. (Proverbs 3:9-10)

I was young and now I am old, yet I have never seen the righteous forsaken or their children begging bread. They are always generous and lend freely; their children will be blessed. (Psalm 37:25-26)

No one can serve two masters. Either you will hate the one and love the other, or you will be devoted to the one and despise the other. You cannot serve both God and money. (Matthew 6:24)

Keep your lives free from the love of money and be content with what you have, because God has said, "Never will I leave you, never will I forsake you." So we say with confidence, "The Lord is my helper, I will not be afraid. What can man do to me?" (Hebrews 13:5-6)

Be shepherds of God's flock that is under your care, serving as overseers—not because you must, but because you are willing, as God wants you to be; not greedy for money, but eager to serve, not lording it over those entrusted to you, but being examples to the flock. And when the Chief Shepherd appears, you will receive the crown of glory that will never fade away. (1 Peter 5:2-4)

Give, and it will be given to you. A good measure, pressed down, shaken together, and running over, will be poured into your lap. For with the measure you use, it will be measured to you. (Luke 6:38)

Food For Thought: *What part does money play in your life? If God prompted your heart to use your money in some way, would you hear Him? Would you act on His prompting? Pray and ask God to help you understand the role of money in your life.*

Rejoice!

Be happy! In God, you have security and hope for the future! Trust him, come to him with your problems, and he will give you a joyful heart.

Rejoice in the Lord always. I will say it again: Rejoice! (Philippians 4:4)

Do not be anxious about anything, but in every situation, by prayer and petition, with thanksgiving, present your requests to God. And the peace of God, which transcends all understanding, will guard your hearts and your minds in Christ Jesus. (Phillipians 4:6)

I delight greatly in the Lord; my soul rejoices in my God. For he has clothed me with garments of salvation and arrayed me in a robe of righteousness, as a bridegroom adorns his head like a priest, and a bride adorns herself with jewels. (Isaiah 61:10)

Rejoice always, pray continually, give thanks in all circumstances; for this is God's will for you in Christ Jesus. (1 Thessalonians 5:16-18)

Those who sow in tears will reap with songs of joy. He who goes out weeping, carrying seed to sow, will return with songs of joy, carrying sheaves with him. (Psalm 126:5,6)

Blessed are those who have learned to acclaim you, who walk in the light of your presence, O Lord. They rejoice in your name all day long; they exult in your righteousness. (Psalm 89:15,16)

I have told you these things so that you may have peace. In this world you will have trouble. But take heart! I have overcome the world. (John 16:33)

Food For Thought: *Take moments in your day to stop, let go of your burdens, and focus on God's greatness. Rejoice in the beauty and majesty of His creation. Rejoice that He is bigger than your problems. Sing a praise song (in your head if you're not in an appropriate place!) or read a Psalm or two. God is present in the praises of His people. Invite Him into your heart whenever you can!*

Forgiveness

Forgiveness is something God takes very seriously. When we hold on to the pain we have experienced as a result of interactions with others, when we hold on to resentment, it gets in the way of our relationship with God.

The Lord knows you have been hurt. He knows the pain of undeserved abuse. He was without fault, yet was crucified.

God asks you to trust him, and leave justice to him. He knows the hearts of those who have abused you. He knows every action they have taken against you. He is the perfect judge.

Please, let go of the pain and leave it with him, so that you can experience the life he has planned for you.

Do not repay evil for evil. Be careful to do what is right in the eyes of everybody. If it is possible, as far as it depends on you, live at peace with everyone. Do not take revenge, my friends, but leave room for God's wrath, for it is written: "It is mine to avenge, I will repay," says the Lord. (Romans 12:17-19)

Do not judge, and you will not be judged. Do not condemn, and you will not be condemned. Forgive, and you will be forgiven. (Luke 6:37)

So watch yourselves. If your brother sins, rebuke him, and if he repents, forgive him. If he sins against you seven times in a day, and seven times comes back to you and says, "I repent," forgive him. (Luke 17:3-4)

For if you forgive men when they sin against you, your heavenly Father will also forgive you. But if you do not forgive men their sins, your Father will not forgive your sins. (Matthew 6:14-15)

Food For Thought: *Forgiving someone is often the hardest thing we ever have to do in life. And as you see, God doesn't give us a choice. Why would He do this? Ask God to help you understand this difficult command.*
Do you have someone you need to forgive, and just can't seem to do it? Maybe you can't even get to the point that you're <u>*trying*</u> *to forgive that person. Ask for God's help, so that you can be set free from the pain of this offense, and can rejoice in God's healing power.*

Temptation

We live in a fallen world. Good and evil coexist on earth. The enemy of the Lord is jealous of you, and would like nothing more than to steal your hope and joy by leading you astray. He will try to tempt you and discourage you with his lies.

All of your life, again and again, you will have opportunities to make a choice of whom you will follow. Learn to follow the Lord's ways. Seek his help when the temptation to turn away is strong.

He will help you to do what is right, no matter how difficult. Just remember to ask for his help, his strength. You will learn that you can trust him. His ways will set you free.

No temptation has seized you except what is common to man. And God is faithful; He will not let you be tempted beyond what you can bear. But when you are tempted, He will also provide a way of escape to that you can stand up under it. (1 Corinthians 10:13)

Submit yourselves, then, to God. Resist the devil, and he will flee from you. Come near to God and he will come near to you. Wash your hands, you sinners, and purify your hearts, you double-minded. Grieve, mourn and wail. Change your laughter to mourning and your joy to gloom. Humble yourselves before the Lord, and he will lift you up. (James 4:7-10)

As for you, you were dead in your transgressions and sins, in which you used to live when you followed the ways of this world and the ruler of the kingdom of the air, the spirit who is now at work in those who are disobedient. All of us also lived among them at one time, gratifying the cravings of our sinful nature and following its desires and thoughts. Like the rest, we were, by nature, objects of wrath. But because of his great love for us, God, who is rich in mercy, made us alive with Christ even when we were dead in transgressions—it is by grace you have been saved...through faith—and this is not from yourselves; it is the gift of God—not by works, so that no one can boast. For we are God's workmanship, created in Christ Jesus to do good works, which God prepared in advance for us to do. (Ephesians 2:1-5,8b-10)

When tempted, no one should say, "God is tempting me." For God cannot be tempted by evil, nor does he tempt anyone: but each one is tempted when, by his own evil desire, he is dragged away and enticed. Then, after desire has conceived, it gives birth to sin; and sin, when it is full-grown, gives birth to death. (James 1:13-15)

Seek first His kingdom and His righteousness, and all these things [the food and clothing you need] will be given to you as well. (Matthew 6:33)

Food For Thought: *Ask for God's help and leading in your decisions, large and small. Seek out trustworthy friendships to help you to grow and be strong. Ask God to teach you how to follow Him.*

The Prize

In God's Word you can read about heaven. You can read that the inhabitants of heaven worship him, saying things like "Holy, holy, holy is the Lord God Almighty, who was and is and is to come," and, "Praise and glory and wisdom and thanks and honor and power and strength be to our God forever and ever. Amen!"

Why do they do this? Wouldn't they rather be entertaining themselves with sports, movies, or video games? If heaven was like the world, yes. Life on earth is a struggle, and people seek relief through escape and distraction whenever they can.

But heaven is different. God's people rejoice because they have been released of their daily struggle. And more than that. They worship him because they are with him, because they know him, because they fully experience his great love and great power, and his holiness, which banishes all evil.

In the world, people have to take the good with the bad. But in heaven, there is no evil. "Holy" means "separate" or "set apart." Evil is far away. God's heaven is untainted by disease, sorrow, selfishness, and pride that causes pain and breaks relationships.

The relief from pain and the joy of his love and acceptance cause his people to burst forth in praise and worship. Heaven is a place of joy and celebration that will not end.

Never again will they hunger; never again will they thirst. The sun will not beat upon them, nor any scorching heat. For the

Lamb at the center of the throne will be their shepherd; he will lead them to springs of living water. And God will wipe away every tear from their eyes. (Revelation 7:16-17)

Then I saw a new heaven and a new earth, for the first heaven and the first earth had passed away, and there was no longer any sea. I saw the Holy City, the new Jerusalem, coming down out of heaven from God, prepared as a bride, beautifully dressed for her husband. And I heard a loud voice from the throne saying, "Now the dwelling of God is with men, and he will live with them. They will be his people, and God himself will be with them and be their God. He will wipe every tear from their eyes. There will be no more death or mourning or crying or pain, for the old order of things has passed away." He who was seated on the throne said, "I am making everything new!" Then he said, "Write this down, for these words are trustworthy and true." He said to me: "It is done. I am the Alpha and the Omega, the Beginning and the End. To him who is thirsty I will give to drink without cost from the spring of the water of life. He who overcomes will inherit all this, and I will be his God and he will be my son. But the cowardly, the unbelieving, the vile, the murderers, the sexually immoral, those who practice magic arts, the idolaters and all liars—their place will be in the fiery lake of burning sulfur. This is the second death. (Revelation 21:1-8)

Behold, I will create new heavens and a new earth. The former things will not be remembered, nor will they come to mind. But be glad and rejoice forever in what I will create, for I will create Jerusalem to be a delight and its people a joy. I will rejoice over Jerusalem and take delight in my people; the sound of weeping and of crying will be heard in it no more. (Isaiah 65:17-19)

In my Father's house are many rooms...I am going there to prepare a place for you. (John 14:2)

Food For Thought: *When we have our eyes on a goal, we are better able to prioritize our actions in order to reach that goal. Ask God to give you a vision for your life, a picture of His purpose for you, and anticipation for the prize you will receive at the end of your journey in this world.*

Wild Stories

Live the life that God wants you to live, and you're going to have some wild stories to tell. Crazy, amazing stories! I suggest you start keeping a journal of them because you'll want to remember the moments, and details can fade quickly in the barrage of thoughts that come afterwards. ("Did that really just happen? That must have just been [fill in the blank with some possible natural cause, no matter how unlikely].")

Here are some of my wild stories where God showed up in a way that was unmistakably out of this world.

One morning I woke up with a tremendous sense of peace, and the idea that I would not die in a car accident. I thought, "Ok, wow, good to know." A few months later, my husband and I were driving south on I-5 in five lanes of Friday night traffic moving at a decent speed. The car on our left came into our lane and the mirror made a crunching noise. The steering was affected; we could not drive straight, could only swerve right. Somehow the traffic in the three lanes to the right suddenly cleared as we went uncontrollably in that direction. The edge of the road dropped off into a ditch, then rose to a hill. The nose of our car went down into the ditch, causing the car to flip over onto the roof. Ridiculously, neither one of us was wearing our seat belts. We both landed on all fours on the inside of the roof, without a scratch.

Many of my wild stories have to do with work and job transitions, which seems appropriate, since God often blesses us through the ways we serve others. Just after our oldest son was born, my husband needed to take a graduate internship as the next step in his career. My employer at the time gave me a really generous offer to stay behind a little while longer to train someone, and in return would pay for trips to our new city on weekends to look for a new job or a place to live. Halfway through the process I could tell that he had surprised himself at what he had offered me, because he asked me, "What did I offer you again?" When I told him, he shook his head and said with raised eyebrows and an incredulous smile, "Well, okay!"

I contacted a recruitment firm in the new city before moving. They found a placement for me which seemed like a good fit at the right salary but it was slow in happening. I started listening to the voices in my head that said I needed to increase my odds by interviewing for other jobs as well. I only succeeded in making myself sick over pursuing additional opportunities. God used an interview discussion about a past failure to show me I just needed to trust him for the first job that was lined up. Sure enough, it came through, and at the perfect time that gave me time to find the right day care and get settled and ready to work.

Two years later, my husband's internship was up, and it was time for him to find another position, likely in another city. He interviewed for several positions in various cities, and not much was happening. It was hard to understand because his work was very specialized and he had gained good experience. We prayed with our small group, who were amazing and encouraging. Still nothing was happening. We felt like it was the end of the road with nowhere to go. My husband finished his internship with no idea what would happen next.

On his first day home, he decided to pack, because no matter what happened, we would have to move. We talked at lunchtime, and he told me he just had to give it to God, because he didn't know what else he could do. That afternoon, he got a call inviting him back to where he had last worked, in the most unlikely position that he had only applied for because he thought he should. They wanted to hire him instead of conducting a wider search that they normally would, because time was short and they knew his work.

Not only was this great news for his career, but it was great for mine as well. My company, which I loved, had another office in our home city and the person in my position, which I also loved, was not working out. And we got to move home! Win-win-win!

Three years and one more son later, life was crazy busy. Every day was all about making it through to the next day. My husband travelled a lot with work, and I was holding down the fort by myself much of the time. I was worn out. I prayed, "God, we don't have time for you, and we don't have time for each other. I don't know how to change this, but I know you can."

My husband called me one day at work and told me about a position he was interested in, half the country away, in a small town, two hours from an airport. We decided to do what we by now had gotten in the habit of doing, which was to fill out the application and pray, "God, if this is a good way to go with you, please open this door. If not, please close it."

He applied, he interviewed, we waited. He called me at work to tell me he got the job. That was it. We were moving to a town that was 11 square miles, no rush hour, and full of friendly faces, we would find out. I put down the phone, and glanced at the scripture calendar I had on my desk. It read, "In my distress I called to the Lord, and he answered me." (Jonah 2:2) A peace that was not of myself filled my upper body in that moment, and I knew that I had been heard, and I had received my answer.

I started working at a place whose financial processes were stalled and cash wasn't coming in as it should. I worked with the director to get things going. It was in an industry new to me so I had a lot to learn. Many days I sat at my desk and prayed, "Lord, I don't know what needs to be done now, but you do. Bring it to my attention, please. We need your help." For my efforts and attitude, I guess, I was voted Employee of the Quarter, and then Employee of the Year.

A new director came in, from a similar industry but from an area where revenue was much less volatile. After nine months, this director went back to her old position, and put me on probation at the same time, assigning half a dozen reports that needed to be prepared and submitted to the board of directors weekly and monthly.

I sat with her and the board president and listened to the terms of my probation. A peace came over me that I could not explain. I knew that things would be okay. I listened, was calm and understanding, and did my best in the coming days to comply with what was requested.

Two or three days later, it dawned on me that I should probably look in the paper to see what positions were out there. Almost immediately, a great one caught my attention. It would allow me to be more focused on two areas of responsibility instead of five, had great benefits, and would increase my salary significantly. It was as if light was streaming from the page, and angels were singing! I applied and got the job. I learned that sometimes, I am the right person for the job in one season, but that season can pass, and it's okay. There will be a new assignment on the way.

Prayer for Salvation

Lord, I confess to you that I have tried to build a life on my own without you, my Creator. I confess that I have not honored you in my life. I humble myself before you now, and thank you for the life you have given me, all the talents you have given me, and all that you have provided for me this far.

I see that I am a sinner, that I have been selfish and self-serving, and that you are calling me to a life that is different. Thank you for showing me that you have a different plan for my life, one in which I will fulfill all of the potential you have for me, in which I will use my gifts to bring you glory instead of myself, and in which I will find the joy and peace that you have meant for me.

Thank you, Lord Jesus, for shedding your blood in payment for my sins, past, present, and future. Thank you for your mercy on me, enabling me to step forward from this day on, walking in your grace and provision, showing me the new life you have for me, one day at a time.

Lead me each day, Lord Jesus. Be my shepherd. Let me hear your voice through your word. When I am joyful, I will praise you. When I am troubled, I will turn to you. When I am afraid, I will trust that you have my life, and the lives of those I love, securely in your hands. When I am tempted to sin, I will remember that you have something better for me, and I will look for the way of escape that you have promised to provide for me. Thank you for your promise to lead me and guide me,

and to provide for my needs. Be glorified through my life, and teach me to walk in your ways.
    Amen.

My Playlist

Beyond Me - TobyMac
Steal My Show - TobyMac
Move (Keep Walkin') - TobyMac
Burn for You - TobyMac
Dare You To Move - Switchfoot
If You Want Me To - Ginny Owens
New Day - Danny Gokey
Haven't Seen It Yet - Danny Gokey
More - Matthew West
Strong Enough - Matthew West
Brave - Moriah Peters
You Carry Me - Moriah Peters
Fix My Eyes - For King and Country
Shoulders - For King and Country
God Only Knows - For King and Country
Unfinished - Mandisa
Overcomer - Mandisa
Even So Come - Kristian Stanfill and Passion
You Say - Lauren Daigle
First - Lauren Daigle
Brave - Nichole Nordeman
Holy - Nichole Nordeman

Favorite Quick Reads

Epic - John Eldredge
A Life God Rewards - Bruce Wilkinson
Secrets of the Vine - Bruce Wilkinson
It's Not About Me - Max Lucado
Uninvited - Lysa TerKeurst
Miracles – Eric Metaxas